THE MIST MEN
and other poems

GEORGE MENDOZA

Decorations by Paul Bacon

THE MIST MEN
and other poems

Doubleday & Company, Inc., Garden City, New York

OTHER BOOKS BY GEORGE MENDOZA

Allegories

AND AMEDEO ASKED, HOW DOES ONE BECOME A MAN? / THE PUMA AND THE PEARL / A PIECE OF STRING / FLOWERS AND GRASSES AND WEEDS / THE HUNTER, THE TICK AND THE GUMBEROO / THE PRACTICAL MAN / THE INSPECTOR.

Poetry

THE HUNTER I MIGHT HAVE BEEN / THE SAND POEMS / TO SEE A TRAIN GO BY / AND I MUST HURRY FOR THE SEA IS COMING IN / FISH IN THE SKY / TIME IS BUT THE STREAM I GO A-FISHING IN / A POEM FOR PUTTING TO SEA / THE STARFISH TRILOGY / THE SCRIBBLER / THE RAINBOW EATER / DREAM POEMS.

and Books for All Ages

HERMAN'S HAT / GWOT! HORRIBLY FUNNY HAIRTICKLERS / THE CRACK IN THE WALL and other terribly weird tales / THE GILLYGOOFANG / A WART SNAKE IN A FIG TREE / THE BEASTLY ALPHABET BOOK / THE DIGGER WASP / THE CATERPILLAR MAN / THE GOOD LUCK SPIDER and other bad luck stories / BIG FROG, LITTLE POND / THE MARCEL MARCEAU ALPHABET BOOK / ARE YOU MY FRIEND? / THE CHRISTMAS TREE ALPHABET BOOK / THE FEARSOME BRAT / THE HAWK IS HUMMING, a novel / HUNTING SKETCHES, short stories / THE WORLD FROM MY WINDOW.

"As Though I Were A Thief With Time" originally appeared under the title "Song to the Battenkill" in the Fall 1969 issue of *The American Sportsman* (Volume 2, Number 4).

"The Hunter I Might Have Been" © by George Mendoza, 1968. Reprinted by permission of: Astor-Honor, Inc., New York, New York 10017

LIBRARY OF CONGRESS CATALOG CARD NUMBER 70-113073

DESIGNED BY EARL TIDWELL

for my sister, Elise,
a long ago promise . . .

*S*UDDENLY the road gets narrow
and lumpy,
winding around.
Stones sit on hills
like scattered villages
and I know the river is near:
Vermont *fifty miles an hour.*

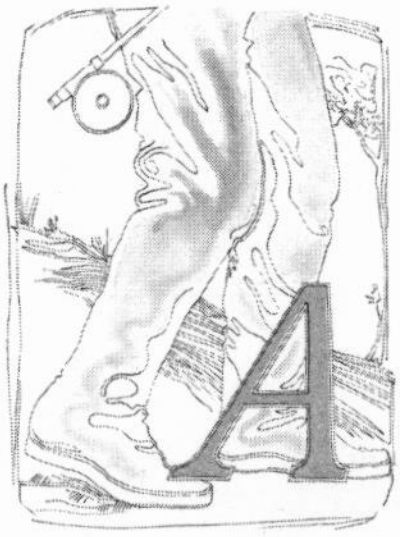

*A*CROSS the meadow-wide
pressing leaves
    down to the turtle stones,
fisherman's boots,
waking the morning, turning the world,
tuning the grass.

*A*LL night
with his cane and his leg stiff
he fished the deeps and shallows of the river.
Like a bat he stalked the bold browns
that foraged for frogs and mice along the banks.

All night
he lived to feel the pluck of his honey-spider fly.
Floating it out in the dark he felt it drift down
in moonless currents as though it were his own heart
and with his fingers feeling the pulse of the line
he spoke to the little stars,
spoke to them all night
till they went out.

*W*HEN time was a boy
I brought the summer earth humming
to my head
and looked at a mountain
through a blade of grass.
The blade of grass, I saw, was taller than the
mountain.
The blade of grass, I dreamed, was taller than the
world.
So I picked it and stuffed it in my pocket,
a mountain and a world.

HE SKY, the woods, the stars
are boulders,
but pebbles, pebbles seem older.

COVERING the brook
a cocoon of mist.
Where is the sun
that will hatch it?

*T*O come upon a tree, such a tree,
braced and packed, cement in her
squirrel hollows,
trunk-scarred, blackened with paint.
Up high her leaves are wet,
her boughs old and stiff.
But round the tree in the young soft grass
as sweet as Spring
are pebbles, pebbles in the grass,
little white pebbles tooting at time like children
playing,
while old roots gnarl the wind.

_I_'M a man with an itch
not in my heart
but in my feet.
When I'm hucking in Vermont
stuffing leaves in my pocket
tying flies to my leader
in the beam of my _Eveready_ in the dark
I'm thinking too soon of the city.
When I'm too long in the city
I'm hucking to get back to Vermont...

                              to Vermont...

stuffing leaves in my pocket
tying flies to my leader
listening to the swish of my rod in the dark.
I'm a man with an itch
with both feet in my heart.

THE ROAD splitting dirt
between two fields
high, once high,
moon in the wheat.
Below the iron bridge
we go:
two boys lost,
looking for downstream dreams.

W E were two little people
drifting in our boat
across the pond
casting three flies a-time for rainbows,
when the thunder rolled, rumbling over the
mountain.
"Can you hear the rain?" I said to my wife
as she looked up to the mountain.
"Listen . . ." she said
and the birches turned their leaves silvery in the
dark.
"It's coming . . ."
"We'd better go back" I said, feeling the first
drops of rain reach us.
"Let it!" She laughed
and we drifted under the angry clouds
licking rain like sweet sap from the bark
of our faces.

I'D like to say
c'mon let's go,
let's hit the road
we'll take our chances,
you got some left?
We'll live like sparrows
for a little less fat!

I come to this mystical brook-river
to escape awhile . . .
      to take my drink as though I were a thief
with time . . .
to dream out dreams,
to cloud my head in clouds
tumbling down like milkweed suns,
to tie a speck of winged fly
to a leader silken as a fair girl's hair,
to walk across fresh-cut fields of rye and wheat
toward a stretch the poet Soper said
was fast and deep,
as sun-gold as the tasseled corn,
to talk to my poet friend
under a sickle of moon, with stars
dusting themselves
and spanning the yards of the dipper.
O let the world spin old
my dawn is sweet,
September cold—
The mist is creeping low,
like a serpent with its head under a rock,
and its tail still weaving in the grass.
On the brook before a flower opens

I'm casting by the dam,
old dam, weather-planked by the burned-down mill
where yellow butterflies flutter
above charred timbers
and wild trout lilies and boneset and mint
tilt like windmills by the stream
and clover balls pop like little plums
in the brush weed.

The smell of the brook is swimming in my head;
my soul reaches for a somewhere prayer.
I know the lunkers are nymphing from the deeps,
but before the morning wind is up
I'll be wandering like a gypsy boy
down the stretch below,
where the white house high on the birch bank
peeps through the pealing trees,
where all the river bends like a bough
and the alder leaves drop in the laughing furrows
to ride and play beside my fly.

'M a dream time man
when the mayfly flies,
caught in a crooked dance
between fish and bird,
beating with the brook my day-night song
till the sky can't hold me
and I'm a swallowed up, juicy bug.

UMMER'S coming,
the sky sows it:
the nest is empty.
Only horse hair and cow hair
pecked from rutted fields remain
where the first feathers
had felt the wind
and little hot bellies pressed close,
like three children lost in snow,
and black eyes went blinking and
beaks opened for peeping.
Now the egg-like crater
cradles summer in the nest
and around it twigs
carved from air.

*A*RE grasses exclamation points
and stones periods?
Are birds grammarians
when they peck with their beaks?
Oh, look to wild weeds
and see how lovely they grow.

I dream under banks of dreams;
by deep pool beds I'll lay my head
and let my dreams flow between mountains,
past springs nippling under fern,
till darkness presses darkness
and all the night
is a river to the stars.

*A*NOTHER hundred years and the river
will be gone:
     stones will look like cattle skulls,
bones of birch will worm the sky,
banks cool in waves of fern
no poet will come to find.
Minnows will not fill the dreams
of a little boy's tobacco can.
Once-vermilion pools of trout,
will lie grave-under,
a wider road to travel on.

HE BAT went wheeing under the bridge,
up stream, down stream,
    back and forth.
It was dark;
I couldn't see the water,
I couldn't see the rocks,
I couldn't see my line
swishing back and forth;
was the bat fishing for me?

SK me what a poem is for
or what it should do
and I would tell you
go plough your hill
while I leave mine wild to grow.

HEN I was a boy,
barely tall,
I shot a sparrow from a tree.
I held its limp body in my hands
and buried it still warm in the soft earth.
Then I fled.
I never touched a gun again.
But years came later when I was a man
I wondered,
oh, the hunter I might have been
had I but met a lion that first day
and not stilled that gentle sparrow's call.

HIS is the place he had disappeared:
he had waded through the meadow
of grasses
beneath a fair, star-flowered night.
Plunging through grasses grown taller
than his years
he had never seen the sudden drop
down to the silt-mud of the oxbow brook.
He was never found; but he was talked about
by waitresses in roadstops for a few days.

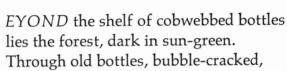

EYOND the shelf of cobwebbed bottles
lies the forest, dark in sun-green.
Through old bottles, bubble-cracked,
the forest splinters
in a sea of pine-boughs,
webbing the wind,
blurring old bottles like old eyes.

*T*HIS is where I go,
down the rapid flashing stretch,
into the winding swirl of stream
where the world wheels on a spool of dreams
and shadows are flowers that never stop opening
and clouds sail out of shells of clouds
and rainbows are the colors of butterfly wings.

 saw three birds
taking a bath
in the park.
One robin,
two common.
The robin flew off,
he was first;
three commoners stayed
a little longer to bathe.

*T*HE skinny kid
leaped for the leaf;
he thought he could catch it—
one green leaf.
It would fall in its own time
but now, wind-turning,
red-speckled with orange suns spinning,
green still running in its rivers,
it held the bough that bore it.
The skinny kid will kick it
in a week or so
if he has a mind to.

Y heart is like an abandoned railroad track
laid out on the black coal rock,
laid out cold like the blades of steel
that run into the falling sky . . .

IGH up the hawk
breathes on the dead
burned-black bough
as I lay my line
to the rising trout.

I did it deliberately:
slipped and fell and broke my skull.
But I remember my boots filling,
hands brushing slippery stones,
sky buckling in a flight of leaves.
Sweeping into the moon of a pool
I bubbled out a laugh that popped
when it reached the surface.

HE cemetery stones are walking
in the final shadows of the light,
white beneath the village stars,
tilting away to night.

OUTSIDE the wind, outside the wind:
leaves flying from graves
        beneath the sheep-nose trees,
field leaves sailing back to derelict boughs
where apples were once planets to be picked.
Now the wind cracks cold
and night stands in the stars
waiting for snow to stick.

'D like to see you get up here friend
to watch the night walk into the mountains,
to hear a bough brushing a window,
to smell a flower with the wind in its petals,
to touch the fever of the sky
when the red moon maddens the eye;
time you got up here friend
it's getting awful late.

HE trap I set
is not a death-clap
of chain and steel and spring
to crunch a hare's bone,
but the sky's open net
of stars like spoon-dust
gathered on a blinding brook.
O I've sent the sun spinning O
like a marble shot to the pot,
the moon I've scooped up
in my scooper
like a squid in the sea
to light the tails of fireflies,
for the forest takes me deep
where pine and birch and fern
are giant seaweed swaying under,
and the fox, and owl, and hawk and snake
are as fish in a sea of fog.

F the mist men could speak,
if only they could speak,
they would tell of the mute boy,
gypsy boy,
come down from his hill home,
wandering nights alone by the wild brook rocks,
moss-rust rocks.
Spinning his sad river songs
from the birch-speckled bank
he sweetened the rise
of the monster German brown,
hook-jaw native brown
down in the deep pool
under the stone, under the dark
under old Buffum's Bridge on Vermont's
mountain river, Battenkill.

If the mist men could speak,
if only they could speak,
they would tell of the morning
when the stars like buds
fled the fields of their flowers
and old Tom, trout fisherman Tom,

came a-wading with the river trailing.
He stood like a crow,
lone and longing,
old as white sun-stone,
a-casting his dry fly like a drop of honey
drifting in the dream of his eye.
Tom to feel the hook set,
Tom to pluck the fish of fishes,
Tom to haul his heart thrashing to the net.
O for such a catch would he give
all his gold on the moon.
When suddenly it rose
not for the honey
floating the hook
but for an old dream-trapper—
Tom, trout fisherman Tom.

If the mist men could speak,
if only they could speak,
they would tell of the mayfly,
wheat-gold as the dust of a buttercup,
gentle mayfly, poet of the stream,
singing to the river's flute:

I began as an egg
on the bottom of the Battenkill.
I was very shy and had to hide
in the gloom and dark
on the bottom of the Battenkill
till I became a nymph.
Bubbling to the surface top
I set myself free;
A mayfly! A mayfly! Oh me, oh me!
But that deadly eye, that cannibal jaw,
that mighty leap, slashing, breaking—
Mayfly! Mayfly!
Will fly, will sing, no more!

If the mist men could speak,
if only they could speak,
they would tell of the mist-moth,
wings melting white in the moon-wash,
sailing the back of the turtle dove.
Sweeping the glassy rocks
they rode a million suns,
falling on the foam and riffles
till they came to the deep pool
where all the world was a boiling swirl,
gushing to a bone-ribbed grave,
down, down to the belly of that German brown.

If the mist men could speak,
if only they could speak,
they would tell of the little brown bat
steering the helm of a black pirate hat,

three-masted and canvas blowing full.
Cannons raised to port,
cannons raised to starboard,
running in the ghostly late-moon light.
Toward the yawning pool the bow was set,
splitting the river's whiskers in the dark.
Port guns fired; starboard guns blazed.
O the monster brown could not be shaken
but took in one swallow
that brown pirate bat.

If the mist men could speak,
if only they could speak,
they would tell of Jess Hawley and George McGee
up from their graves they laid their stones
leaping and dancing round the old
moss-creeping cemetery
along Vermont's winding river-route 313,
rattling their bones, rat-tat-tat-tat-ling
down the road,
to the old covered bridge
where the moon tonight haunts the hollowed eyes
and the river spills like old woman's lace
over the monster brown's hole.

"Let's swing from the rope under the bridge!" came the
call of the boy still aflame in McGee. "That's how I croaked!"
shouted Hawley. "For breaking poor Bertha's heart I was
sentenced and hung!"

"Ay!" cried McGee. "But they're too rotten in their graves
to do it again!"

So with the wind in their bones
two mad fools swung
into the crater of jaws
that found not a stitch of flesh
revolting.

If the mist men could speak,
if only they could speak,
they would tell of the night,
as they gathered round for a glass of fog,
a black cold spike drove through their hearts.

"It's the panther!" whispered John.
". . . reluctant beast come from his cave for a drink . . ."
hissed Ralph.
"To take his sippin' with the hungry monster brown!"
moaned Matthew.
"Ay, they share one and the same!" echoed the voices of
the mist men.

And the night grew still as the mist men waited,
for the panther was padding silently near.
Till he suddenly appeared like the back of a shadow,
crouching low at the edge of the cannibal's hole.
But none could see the deathly stare
between the little stars like wild seeds
sown in the eyes of beast and fish
or know each was the other
as the wind that moves the rain.

If the mist men could speak,
if only they could speak,

they would sing the song of the mistwind
when the mist comes creeping low
and the moon is afloat like a poppy-balloon
and all the stars are little tumbleweeds
thrown to the night:

       Come up, big brown, come up;
       hear the frogs-turned-witches blow,
       splash with the whippoorwill
       who lives in a whistle
       when the sun is going dark,
       sail under the moonfalls
       that keep the sky on stilts;
       dive, big brown, dive,
       for the mistwind is the moon's wide net
       to drift you from the deep.

. . . with a special feeling for
John Ernst,
    Alex Gotfryd,
      and Earl Tidwell
who saw pebbles in the grass
as galaxies of white clover . . .

GEORGE MENDOZA, a native New Yorker, attended the State University of New York Maritime College for two years and received his B.A. degree from Columbia University. Having always lived near the sea, he learned to sail as a boy and has twice crossed the Atlantic Ocean alone on a small sloop from New York to England. A novelist, poet, and allegorist, he is also the author of a number of books for children and is the winner of a Lewis Carroll Shelf Award. Mr. Mendoza lives in New York City but spends his summers in Vermont haunting the Battenkill River, his favorite trout-fishing ground.